The PORTABLE Mother

The PORTABLE Mother

Stacey Granger

Cumberland House

Nashville, Tennessee

Perhaps it's like that with you and yours. If so, maybe this book is for you. I wrote it to keep alive some memories that had faded, and in the process I came to see my mother in more human terms, as less of an authority figure and more as a person who was more like me than I had ever expected. Likely as not, as a girl she had heard many of these expressions from her own mother.

I've called this book *The Portable Mother*, partly in jest and partly in all seriousness. Truly, we all carry our mothers with us wherever we go, so in that sense they really are portable. And as far as this book is concerned, I like to think that my mother isn't that unlike yours and that occasionally both of us will enjoy a quiet moment when we pull *The Portable Mother* from our purse—or off the coffee table or shelf—and enjoy a memory of a long-past day when she looked us in the eye and said with a tear in her own, "I am *so* proud of you!"

And who knows, as our own children come tearing into the room—laughing or shouting or crying—maybe we will be inspired by a warning that became a prophecy: "When you get older, you'll see I was right."

Introduction

I always thought my brother, sister, and I were just normal, everyday kids, so I was amazed when my mother would yell at us, "I've had it up to here with you kids!" I never could figure out why she was so angry. Neither could my brother or sister.

So we would look at each other like, "What? What'd we do?" We were just doing normal everyday kid things, like playing ball in the house or jumping on the furniture.

Then she would stare at us real hard—we called it the "evil eye"—to let us know just how serious she was, before storming away. It took us only about three seconds, or in her words, "As soon as my back was turned," to go back to being normal, everyday kids again.

Before we knew it, she would be back again, and this time she was even more angry. Funny how the look on her face—never our actions—let us know we were "gonna get it."

Mother was full of such sayings. How many times *did* she complain, "If I've told you once, I've told you a thousand times." Did we just not understand the word *no*? Why else would she have yelled, "Didn't I just tell you no?"

Mother's sayings never meant much to me back then. I was too busy being a child. And once I was grown and on my own, I forgot about them—until *I* became a mother. Then suddenly I *became* my mother! Fully equipped with every last phrase she ever said to me, I suddenly found myself repeating her.

Oh, well, I guess that just blew her theory that everything she ever said "went in one ear and out the other." They must have gotten stuck somewhere in my brain, lying dormant until I gave birth to my first daughter.

So now that I'm my mother, I get to tell *my* kids, "I've had it up to here with you kids!" And she gets to laugh at me.

— Stacey Granger

The
PORTABLE
Mother

Did you change your underwear?

Change your underwear.

Someday you'll thank me.

Because I said so.

How many times
do I have to tell you?

You should know
better than that.

As long as you
live under my roof,
you'll do as I say.

Just you wait
until your father
gets home.

This is just what
I've always wanted!

If I've told you
once, I've told you
a thousand times.

Why don't you put
a little *more* catsup
on your hamburger?

Could you make that
any louder, please?

I want you to sit there
and think about
what you did.

How do you know
you won't like it
until you *taste* it?

Some day you'll
understand.

I told you …

Someday you'll thank me.

Itsy bitsy spider ...

Don't touch that! It's hot!

Eat it. It's good for you.

I know what's best for you.

You're going out
looking like *that*!?

Don't forget to brush
your teeth.

Look both ways before
you cross the street.

I don't care what she does. *You* are my daughter, not her.

Don't swim after you eat, or you'll get cramps.

Because I'm the mom,
that's why.

Make sure you wash
behind your ears.

Mark my words.

You'll poke your eye out.

Next time, ask me first.

Say please.

Look before you leap.

You're going to be the
death of me.

I am *so* proud of you!

I need some peace and
quiet for a change.

How did you get
so dirty!?

What do you mean, you lost it?

I can tell if you're lying.

Don't climb so high.
You might fall.

Let mommy kiss it.

J ust give me one
good reason.

J ust because your friends
do it, doesn't mean
you have to.

Don't leave the refrigerator door open.

Just because it didn't jump out and bite you doesn't mean it's not there.

Don't jump on the bed.

I've got one nerve left, and you're getting on it.

I'm not crying. I've got something in my eye.

I sacrifice everything
for you, and this is the
thanks I get?

You've got more water
on the floor than
in the tub!

Don't put that in your mouth! You don't know where it's been.

Don't swallow those seeds, or you'll grow a watermelon in your stomach.

Mommy will make it
all better.

I promise.

You are so special.

Don't hit.

❧

Clean up this mess!

❧

Don't touch that!

Slow down!

What a big boy you are!

Yes, you only get one dollar
for a hundred pennies.

Don't run in the house.

This is what I cooked,
and you'll eat it.

Who messed this up?

❧

Do you think I'm
made of money?

When I was your age …

Nobody likes a tattle-tail.

Put that back!

I'm not making any promises.

Wipe that look off your face.

Eat your vegetables.
They're good for you.

I cook and I clean . . .

How many times must
I repeat myself?

It'll stop hurting by the time
you're married.

Use your best judgment.

Next time you'll know better.

Get down from there!

Give me that!

Clean it up when you're done.

Trust me.

Practice makes perfect.

I am *so happy* for you!

I don't care who started it.

I only want what's best for you.

When you get older, you'll see I was right.

Go ask your father.

I only have
two hands.

I'm not angry.
I'm just disappointed.

Just because it's different
doesn't make it bad.

Don't stick out your tongue.
It's not nice.

How do you know you
can't unless you try?

Money doesn't
grow on trees!

And I'm quite certain your
father will agree.

No one ever said
growing up was easy.

I'm not making a
special meal just for you.

If you eat any more of
that watermelon, people are
going to start thumping
your stomach.

You're making this harder
than it has to be.

That was good.
Now lets have the truth.

Your teacher does
not hate you.

You can think of a better
excuse than that.

Go to bed.

It's only because
I love you.

For the last time …

Please don't
lick your plate.

How can you live
in this pigsty!?

It's not the
end of the world.

One day
you'll see I was right.

Don't you think
you've had enough?

You can try it,
but I don't think you'll like it.

Don't point.
It's not polite.

Don't talk to strangers.

You got that from your
father's side of the family.

Everyone makes mistakes.

It didn't just get up and
walk away on its own.

Don't give me any excuses.
Just *do* it!

Keep it up, and your face
will freeze like that.

Do your homework.

Wash your face.

Do I make myself clear?

Let me tell you a
thing or two.

We can only hope
for the best.

I'll explain when
you're older.

This will always be
your home.

You'd forget your head if it wasn't attached to your neck.

Tie your shoelaces!

It seems like you were
born just yesterday.

Beauty is only skin deep.

Zip up your coat,
or you'll catch a cold.

You have to take your
medicine if you want
to get better.

Don't "But, Mom" me!

You better be good.
Santa is watching.

Too much TV is bad
for your eyes.

I spent all day slaving
over a hot stove.

You know I would
if I could.

If you start something,
finish it.

I never claimed
to be perfect.

So this is what you call
a clean room?

Nobody ever said
life was fair.

No, you can't have candy.
It's too close to dinner time.

I'm sick and tired . . .

Maybe someday.

Just because.

Do unto others as you would have done unto you.

There's a lesson to be learned from all of this.

Let Mommy show you how.

Pat-a-cake, pat-a-cake,
baker's man . . .

I'm doing the best I can.

Life goes on.

Behave yourself.

Well, I never!

❧

Don't call people names.

❧

Who did *this*?

I fail to see the humor in this.

I don't like this any more
than you do.

Don't use that tone
of voice with me,
young man.

Stop running around like a chicken with its head cut off.

Don't come running to me.

I was your age once.

If you take care of it,
it will last forever.

This is the last straw.

Look it up.

Go to your room.

Stop fighting!

Come in before dark.

Come give me a hug.

You can look, but don't touch.

All that candy will
rot your teeth.

Moms know these things.

All the little pufferbellies
lined up in a row ...

See? Mommy can do it.
Now you try.

Respect your elders.

You're getting too big
for your britches.

There are only so many
hours in a day.

Where did you ever get
that idea?

Someday you'll have kids
of your own.

Would you just
knock it off?

They are called drawers,
and you put things in them.

I'll bet you could
if you tried.

Why can't you do it the
first time I ask?

Well, I'm finished with my homework. What about yours?

Oh, a clean T-shirt! I see you're dressing for dinner this evening..

Don't count your chickens
before they hatch.

Be grateful for what you have.
There are a lot of people less
fortunate than you.

I can dress you up,
but I can't take you out.

Accidents happen.

Remember to say
thank you.

Don't speak with
your mouth full.

Your eyes are bigger
than your stomach.

Not at the table,
you don't!

Do you think I talk just to
hear myself talk?

Let your conscience
be your guide.

I won't always be there
to protect you.

I feel like I'm talking to
a brick wall.

The world does not owe
you a living.

Stand up straight.

Am I getting through
to you?

You are too young.

There is always a first time
for everything.

I'll wash your mouth out
with soap.

Count your blessings.

Nobody is perfect.

Get out of my sight!

If you say you can't,
you never will.

Where did you ever
learn *that*!?

I'd always hoped that someday you would meet a nice boy.

There's no use crying over spilled milk.

Never say never.

We all seem to learn
the hard way.

It could be worse.

I can never get a word
in edgewise.

Get off the phone!

You've got a telephone receiver growing out of your ear.

Your nose has grown a foot in the last 30 seconds.

You're not going to be happy
until someone ends up
getting hurt.

Don't make me
say that again!

What do you mean,
you're a little worried about
your report card?

If at first you don't succeed,
try, try again.

For crying out loud!

When I say no, I mean no.

Shape up or ship out.

Turn off the lights.

Hang up your clothes.

Make your bed.

Eat it. There are people starving
all over the world.

I'm only going to tell you once.

When, exactly, are you going to grow up?

I want an answer,
young man.

And let this be
a lesson to you.

Everything I tell you goes in one ear and out the other.

You just *think* you're smarter than me.

It's only as good
as you make it.

Look at me when I'm
talking to you.

There's no substitute
for a hot bath and
a cup of cocoa.

This is your last warning.

Don't sit so close
to the television.

Don't be in such a hurry
to grow up.

Everything happens
for a reason.

When will you
ever learn?

Save your pennies
for a rainy day.

You get out of it
what you put into it.

Good things come to
those who wait.

You march right in here,
young man!

You're never too old for
hugs and kisses.

Beauty is in the eye
of the beholder.

Every cloud has
a silver lining.

Do you have any jeans
without rips and tears?

What's meant to be
is meant to be.

Maybe you'll remember that
the next time.

That's what you get
when you start trouble.

Don't drink out of
the carton.

Be sure to
take ID with you.

Don't forget to call me
when you get there.

You're treading on
thin ice!

If you can't say something nice,
don't say anything at all.

Good things come
in small packages.

Enjoy your youth.
Someday you'll be as old as me.

Put that down,
and go wash your hands!

It's for your own good.

Close the door.
Were you raised in a barn?

Where have you been?

Don't you sass me!

Don't eat the yellow snow.

Stop whining!

It'll spoil your appetite.

Pick up your socks.

I'm going to count to three
and pull it off. One . . .

Let's get one thing
straight right now.

🌿

You're only young once.

I've had all of this I can stand.

From now on ...

Remember who you are.

Clean your room.

Enough is enough.

Go get a haircut.

No matter how big you get,
you'll always be my baby.

Don't step
in the puddles.

Blood is thicker
than water.

You better listen,
and listen good.

I'm not fooling
around anymore

Be quiet.
I can't hear myself think!

I've had just about
enough of that.

I'm so glad I'm your mom.

The dentist is your *friend*.

Try it. You'll like it.

Please be careful.

When I was your age ...

Save the best for last.

I love you.